# CONTENTS

## Mr. William Shakespeare's
### presented by Marcia Williams

## CREDITS

**Published by Scholastic Ltd,**
Villiers House,
Clarendon Avenue,
Leamington Spa,
Warwickshire CV32 5PR
Text © Huw Thomas
© 2000 Scholastic Ltd
1 2 3 4 5 6 7 8 9 0   0 1 2 3 4 5 6 7 8 9

**Author** Huw Thomas
**Editor** Joel Lane
**Assistant editor** David Sandford
**Series designer** Lynne Joesbury
**Designer** Rachel Warner
**Illustrations** Marcia Williams
**Cover illustration** Marcia Williams

Designed using Adobe Pagemaker

British Library Cataloguing-in-Publication Data
A catalogue record for this book is available
from the British Library.

ISBN 0-439-01761-0

## ACKNOWLEDGEMENTS

**Walker Books Ltd, London** for the use of text and
illustrations from *Mr. William Shakespeare's Plays*
by Marcia Williams © 1998, Marcia Williams (1998,
Walker).

# INTRODUCTION

## *Mr. William Shakespeare's Plays* presented by Marcia Williams

Marcia Williams has retold Greek myths and the stories of King Arthur and Robin Hood. Here's what she said when interviewed about her retelling of Shakespeare's plays.

**Q:** Why did you decide to retell Shakespeare?

**A:** It was something that I had long wanted to do. I felt that most of the retellings of Shakespeare were telling the stories, but not giving the atmosphere of plays. They were written as performances. Also, a lot of the retellings lacked fun. It's not that I think I've retold them better than everyone else, I just have a different approach.

**Q:** How did you get the idea of setting the stories on a stage with an audience?

**A:** When I started doing the book the Globe Theatre had just re-opened in London, and I just went round there with an actor. He described the whole atmosphere of the place so well it really came alive for me. That's when I decided I wanted the audience at the side.

**Q:** Some people think Shakespeare is boring. What do you think?

**A:** Shakespeare was an entertainer and they are just great stories. If you find life dull, then Shakespeare's dull.

# Mr. William who?

● What do you know about William Shakespeare?

**?** When was he born?

**?** What did he write?

**?** Why is he famous?

**?** Where did he live?

**?** What did he look like?

**?** Why do people like his work?

● Make a list of things you know about William Shakespeare.

| Things I know about William Shakespeare |
|---|
|  |
|  |
|  |
|  |
|  |
|  |

# What might happen?

In the book, you will encounter the following situations.

● Where could they lead? Write down what might happen in these stories.

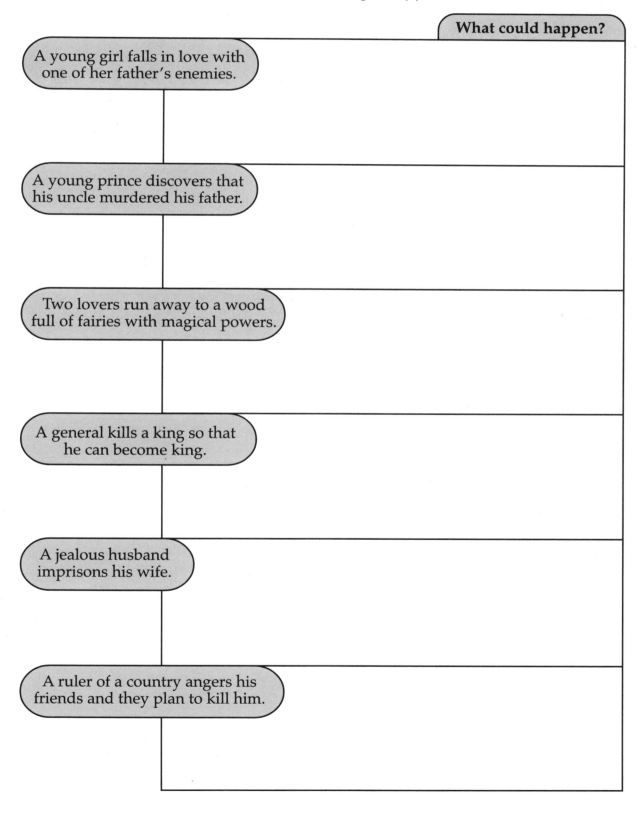

|  | What could happen? |
| --- | --- |
| A young girl falls in love with one of her father's enemies. | |
| A young prince discovers that his uncle murdered his father. | |
| Two lovers run away to a wood full of fairies with magical powers. | |
| A general kills a king so that he can become king. | |
| A jealous husband imprisons his wife. | |
| A ruler of a country angers his friends and they plan to kill him. | |

# Marcia Williams' pages

● Look at what Marcia Williams says about the way her book is organised:

There are three parts to each performance: the words that Shakespeare actually wrote are those spoken by the actors; the story, or plot of the play, is told underneath the pictures; and the spectators, who are famously rude and noisy, can be seen and heard around the stage.

● Now turn to the first page of 'Romeo and Juliet'. Cut out the sentences below, then sort them into three piles:
- words that Shakespeare actually wrote
- words from the story, or plot of the play
- words spoken by spectators.

● Stick the sentences down in three separate groups on a blank sheet of paper.

| | | |
|---|---|---|
| He shall be endur'd. | And her only 13. | Did my heart love till now? |
| Nuts for sale! | Her beauty stole his heart. | Do you bite your thumb at us, sir? |
| He loves her. | Will you be my Juliet? | The quarrel ran so deep that even their servants fought. |
| So Romeo wooed Juliet and soon their love was mutual, despite the feud. | But Lord Capulet was wrong. | Uncle, this is a Montague! |

# If only...

● Read 'Romeo and Juliet'. Think about how the story could have ended differently.
● The list below suggests things that **could** have happened. For each one, write a way in which the story could have been different.

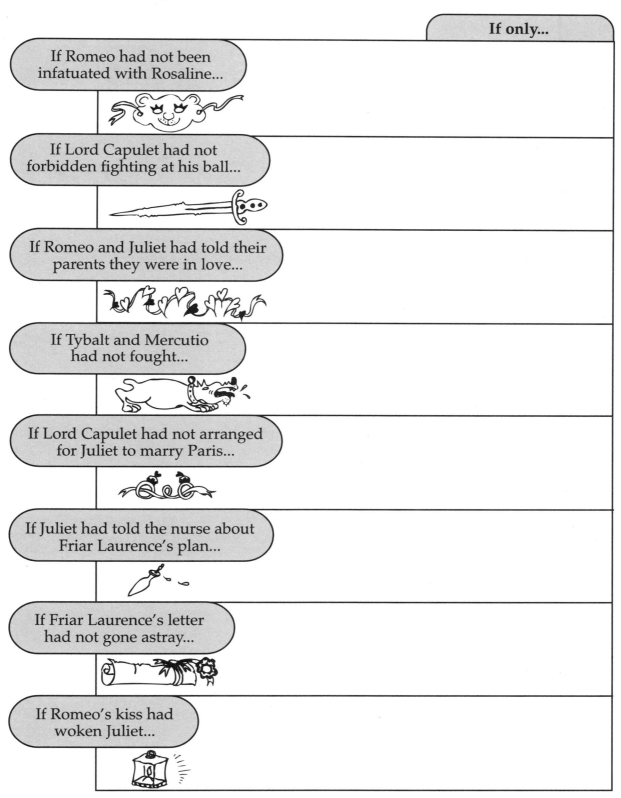

If only...

If Romeo had not been infatuated with Rosaline...

If Lord Capulet had not forbidden fighting at his ball...

If Romeo and Juliet had told their parents they were in love...

If Tybalt and Mercutio had not fought...

If Lord Capulet had not arranged for Juliet to marry Paris...

If Juliet had told the nurse about Friar Laurence's plan...

If Friar Laurence's letter had not gone astray...

If Romeo's kiss had woken Juliet...

# Verona Times

● Cut out the question cards below.
● Work in groups of three. Each of you pretends to be one of these three characters:

Juliet's nurse

Friar Laurence

Lord Capulet

● Place the questions face downwards in the centre of the group.
● Turn the cards over one at a time. They are interview questions being asked by a reporter for the *Verona Times*. Whichever character the question is for has to answer it.

| | | |
|---|---|---|
| **Question for Nurse**<br><br>Why didn't you tell Lord Capulet about Juliet and Romeo? | **Question for Nurse**<br><br>What happened when you tried to wake Juliet? | **Question for Nurse**<br><br>What would you have done if you'd known about Juliet's plan? |
| **Question for Lord Capulet**<br><br>Why did you forbid fighting at your ball? | **Question for Lord Capulet**<br><br>What would you have done if you had found Romeo climbing the orchard wall? | **Question for Lord Capulet**<br><br>Why were you forcing Juliet to marry Paris? |
| **Question for Friar Laurence**<br><br>Why did you agree to marry Romeo and Juliet? | **Question for Friar Laurence**<br><br>How would you have explained Romeo and Juliet's wedding to their families? | **Question for Friar Laurence**<br><br>What plan did you and Juliet make? |

# Trouble at Elsinore

● Read 'Hamlet, Prince of Denmark'.

● Hamlet is a complicated character. What does each of these characters think about him?

Ophelia

Gertrude

Polonius

Claudius

Laertes

Horatio

READ & RESPOND

9

Mr. William Shakespeare's Plays

# Unhappy families

'Hamlet, Prince of Denmark' involves some complicated family problems.

The statements below are written using family titles for characters. For example, Hamlet can be referred to as 'Gertrude's son'.

● Which of the statements are true and which are false? Tick one box next to each statement.

Hamlet's mother married Ophelia's father. **True** ☐ **False** ☐

Gertrude's husband stabbed Horatio's friend. **True** ☐ **False** ☐

Gertrude's son said he once loved Polonius's daughter. **True** ☐ **False** ☐

Hamlet's mother married Hamlet's uncle. **True** ☐ **False** ☐

Hamlet's uncle had a fencing match with Claudius's wife. **True** ☐ **False** ☐

Horatio's friend stabbed Gertrude's husband. **True** ☐ **False** ☐

Ophelia's brother had a fencing match with Claudius's nephew. **True** ☐ **False** ☐

Ophelia's brother spied on Polonius's daughter. **True** ☐ **False** ☐

Ophelia's father spied on Claudius's nephew. **True** ☐ **False** ☐

Polonius's daughter once loved Hamlet's uncle. **True** ☐ **False** ☐

# Who loves who?

● Cut out the question box below.

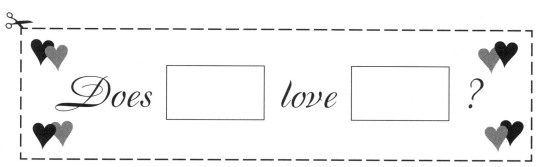

● Cut out the character cards. Place two of them in the question box. For example:

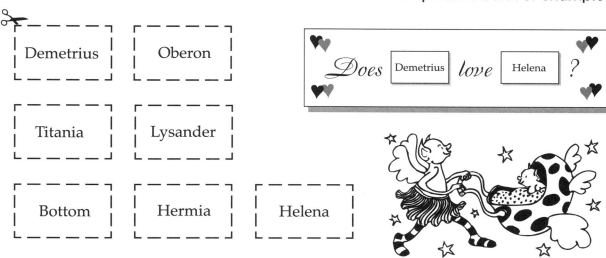

● How many questions can you make that could be answered with 'yes' at some time in 'A Midsummer Night's Dream'? Make a list of them.

# Magic flower

● Can you find four occasions in 'A Midsummer Night's Dream' when magic makes one character fall in love with another?

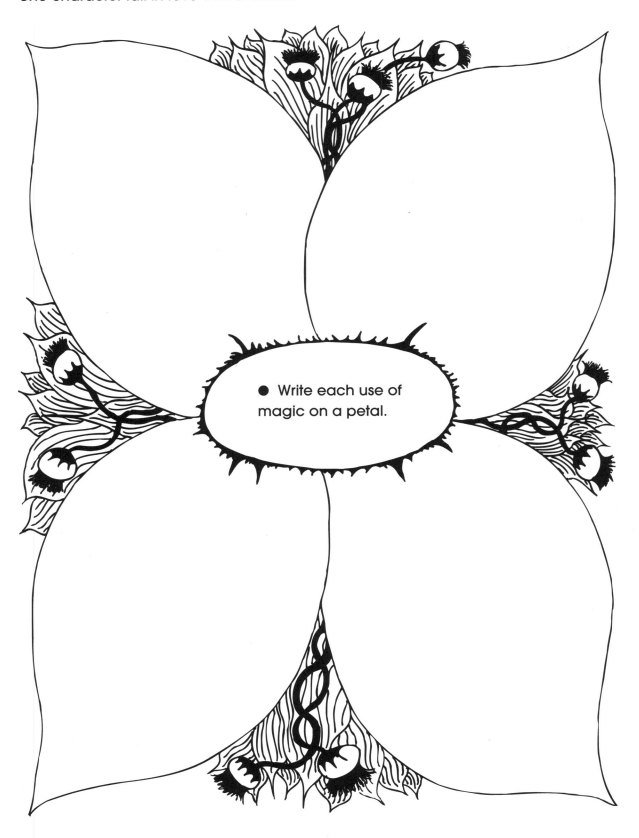

● Write each use of magic on a petal.

# Bad to worse

In the story of 'Macbeth', things get worse and worse for Macbeth.

● Cut out these events. Can you arrange them in order to show how things start well for Macbeth, but then go from bad to worse?

● When you have checked the order, stick the events down on another sheet of paper.

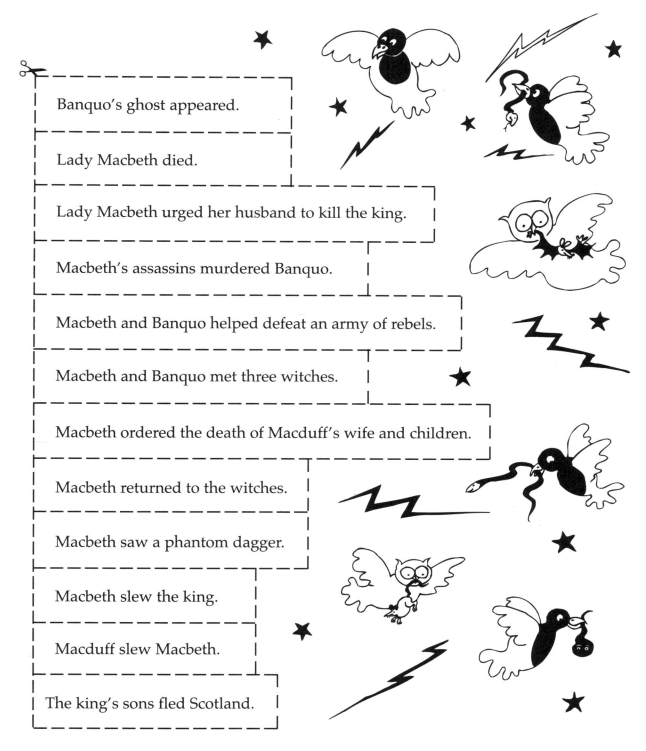

Banquo's ghost appeared.

Lady Macbeth died.

Lady Macbeth urged her husband to kill the king.

Macbeth's assassins murdered Banquo.

Macbeth and Banquo helped defeat an army of rebels.

Macbeth and Banquo met three witches.

Macbeth ordered the death of Macduff's wife and children.

Macbeth returned to the witches.

Macbeth saw a phantom dagger.

Macbeth slew the king.

Macduff slew Macbeth.

The king's sons fled Scotland.

# Audience comments

The audience around the stage say all kinds of things about the plays they watch.
Some of the comments they make about 'Macbeth' are shown below.

● Look at each comment. Write down what event in the play caused this response.

I hope he doesn't believe them.

This is a response to

He's not out of the woods yet.

This is a response to

Typical, says one thing, means another.

This is a response to

Three mugs to crack one nut!

This is a response to

You see, she's all heart, really.

This is a response to

That'll teach her to be naughty.

This is a response to

Thank goodness I brought my smelling salts.

This is a response to

# A cast list

● Look at the list of characters from 'The Winter's Tale' below.

● Read through the story, then note something about each character. It could be a description of the character, or something the character does.

| | |
|---|---|
| Leontes | Hermione |
| Mamillius | Paulina |
| Perdita | Florizel |
| Camillo | Polixenes |

# Leontes' reactions

● Look at how Leontes reacts to some of the things that happen in 'The Winter's Tale'.
● Next to each event listed below, write down Leontes' reaction.

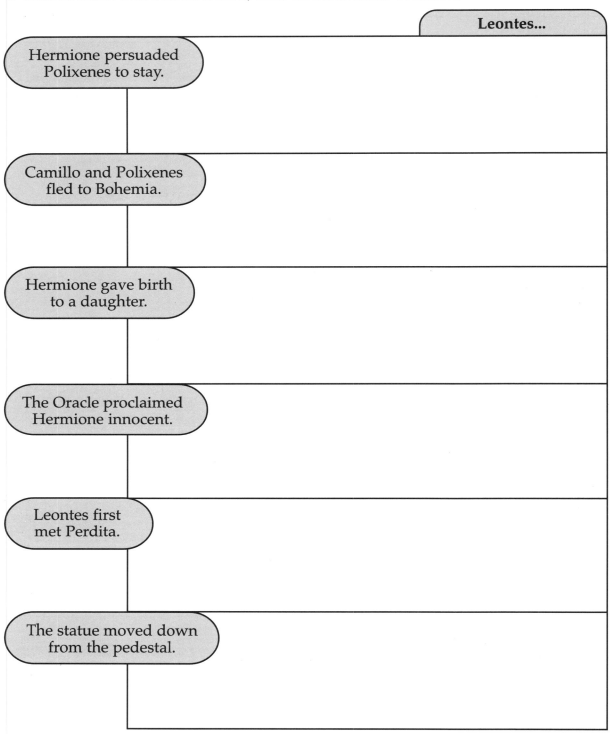

Leontes…

Hermione persuaded Polixenes to stay.

Camillo and Polixenes fled to Bohemia.

Hermione gave birth to a daughter.

The Oracle proclaimed Hermione innocent.

Leontes first met Perdita.

The statue moved down from the pedestal.

● Make some notes on the back of this sheet about:
● what sort of person Leontes was in the early part of the play
● how he changed later on.

# Guess who?

- Work with a partner.
- Look through the story of 'Julius Caesar' together, then close the book.

Here is a list of characters from the story:

| | | | |
|---|---|---|---|
| Mark Antony | Brutus | Calpurnia | Cassius |
| Octavius | Portia | Casca | Soothsayer |

- Without looking at the story again, can you and your partner answer these questions?

Who warned Caesar to beware? _____

Who explained what happened at the games? _____

Who offered Caesar the crown? _____

Who particularly envied Caesar? _____

Who hesitated to join the plot to kill Caesar? _____

Who dreamed of Caesar's death? _____

Who was the last person to stab Caesar? _____

Who was the only one who grieved for Caesar? _____

Who swore to avenge Caesar's death? _____

Who told the people of Rome that Caesar had

threatened their freedom? _____

Who formed an alliance with Mark Antony? _____

Who quarrelled with Brutus? _____

Who committed suicide? _____

Who paid his respects to the dead Brutus? _____

# An argument

In this scene from 'Julius Caesar', Brutus and Cassius have a big row about money.
● A fuller version of the scene from Shakespeare's play is given below. Underline the words from the argument which appear in Marcia Williams' version.
● Read through the scene given below with a partner, one of you playing Brutus and the other Cassius.

**Brutus**  Let me tell you, Cassius, you yourself
Are much condemn'd to have an itching palm;
To sell and mart your offices for gold
To undeservers.

**Cassius**  I an itching palm?
You know, that you are Brutus that speak this,
Or, by the gods, this speech were else your last.

**Brutus**  Go to; you are not, Cassius.

**Cassius**  I am.

**Brutus**  I say, you are not.

**Cassius**  Urge me no more, I shall forget myself:
Have mind upon your health; tempt me no further.

**Brutus**  There is no terror, Cassius, in your threats;
For I am arm'd so strong in honesty
That they pass by me as the idle wind,
Which I respect not. I did send to you
For certain sums of gold, which you denied me;
or I can raise no money by vile means.

**Cassius**  I denied you not.

**Brutus**  You did.

**Cassius**  I did not: he was but a fool
That brought my answer back. You love me not.

**Brutus**  I do not like your faults.

**Cassius**  A friendly eye could never see such faults.

**Brutus**  A flatterer's would not, though they do appear
As huge as high Olympus.

**Cassius**  Come, Antony, and young Octavius, come,
Revenge yourselves alone on Cassius,
For Cassius is aweary of the world:
Hated by one he loves; brav'd by his brother;
There is my dagger,
And here my naked breast; within, a heart.

**Brutus**  Sheathe your dagger:
Be angry when you will, it shall have scope.

**Cassius**  Hath Cassius lived
To be but mirth and laughter to his Brutus,
When grief, and blood ill-temper'd, vexeth him?

**Brutus**  When I spoke that, I was ill-temper'd too.

**Cassius**  Do you confess so much? Give me your hand.

**Brutus**  And my heart too.

# Points of view

● Read 'The Tempest'. Think about the characters.

● In the boxes below, write down what each pair of characters think of each other. If the story doesn't tell you, you can still have a guess.

| | |
|---|---|
| Prospero | Caliban |
| Caliban | Ariel |
| Miranda | Prospero |
| Ferdinand | Miranda |
| Ariel | Alonso |
| Alonso | Prospero |
| Miranda | Alonso |
| Ariel | Prospero |

# Moment jigsaws

THE TEMPEST

● Cut out the jigsaw pieces below. Each one shows a moment of the story that connects with another moment. They have been split up.
● Match each jigsaw piece to its partner. Stick the moment pairs on a sheet of blank paper, in the order in which they happened.

After Ferdinand followed Ariel's singing,

When Miranda suspected her father caused the storm,

Prospero revealed how they were cast away on the island.

Prospero pretended to accuse him of spying.

Trinculo hid under Caliban's cloak,

To seal the bond of Ferdinand's love for Miranda,

he fell in love with Miranda.

then Stefano fell over them both.

To scare away Trinculo, Stefano and Caliban,

When Alonso, Antonio and Gonzalo were about to eat,

Prospero unleashed a pack of phantom hounds.

Ariel made the food vanish.

Before Prospero left the island,

When they saw Prospero,

he released Ariel.

Antonio and Alonso begged to be forgiven.

Mr. William Shakespeare's Plays

READ & RESPOND

20

Photocopiable

# Lines and plays

● Look at these lines from the seven plays. Find out who said each line and why.

| | Who said it? | Why? |
|---|---|---|
| Parting is such a sweet sorrow | | |
| All hail, Macbeth, that shall be king hereafter! | | |
| But are they, Ariel, safe? | | |
| I do fear the people Choose Caesar for their king. | | |
| I love thee not, therefore pursue me not. | | |
| Mother, you have my father much offended. | | |
| My wife is slippery? | | |
| Good Capulet, which name I tender as dearly as my own. | | |
| Chide me, dear stone, that I may say indeed Thou art Hermione. | | |
| Gertrude, do not drink. | | |
| If this prove A vision of the island, one dear son Shall I twice lose. | | |
| O, treachery! Fly, good Fleance, fly, fly, fly! Thou mayst revenge. | | |
| Et tu, Brute? | | |
| What thou seest, when thou dost wake, Do it for thy true-love take. | | |

# Character groups

● Cut out these characters.
● Can you sort them into the seven plays in which they appeared?

| | | |
|---|---|---|
| Antony | Banquo | Caesar |
| Caliban | Cassius | Claudius |
| Hamlet | Helena | Friar Laurence |
| Hermione | Juliet | Lady Macbeth |
| Leontes | Macbeth | Miranda |
| Prospero | Oberon | Ophelia |
| Perdita | Puck | Romeo |

● Can you make different groupings out of these characters? For example, you might sort them into:
● good and bad characters
● funny and serious characters.

# Common features

● Think about the seven Shakespeare plays retold in this book. Are there some themes which appear in more than one play?

● Can you find two plays that share each of these themes?

Two plays in which sons or daughters disagree with their parents.

Two plays in which kings are murdered.

Two plays with ghosts.

Two plays in which magic is used.

Two plays in which one character thinks another is dead – but she isn't.

Two plays in which characters are warned about the future.

Two plays in which plays are acted out.

Two plays in which characters run away.

# Stages and balconies

● Use these picture boxes to draw five events from Shakespeare plays, including quotes from the characters. You can take these from the book, or write your own. Write a description of the event under each picture.

● Now use the balcony boxes to draw your own audience members in the style of Marcia Williams. Decide what they might say and write it in speech bubbles.

READ & RESPOND

Photocopiable

# A Shakespeare quiz

● Work with two friends. Cut out the question cards and place them face down on the table.

● Pick up one question at a time. As a team, try to answer as many as you can without looking at the book.

| | | | | |
|---|---|---|---|---|
| Who did Romeo love? | In 'The Winter's Tale', what was the name of Leontes' wife? | In 'A Midsummer Night's Dream', why did Oberon and Titania argue? | What was the name of Hamlet's mother? | Where did Macbeth live? |
| In 'A Midsummer Night's Dream', who did Hermia love? | Name the friar who married Romeo and Juliet. | Who told Hamlet his father had been murdered? | In 'The Tempest', who was Miranda's father? | What did the soothsayer warn Julius Caesar? |
| Who did Lord Capulet want Juliet to marry? | Who grieved for Julius Caesar? | Who became King after Macbeth? | In 'The Tempest', who fell over Trinculo and Caliban? | Who did Duke Theseus marry in 'A Midsummer Night's Dream'? |
| In 'Julius Caesar', why did Brutus and Cassius quarrel? | What happened to the 'statue' of Hermione? | Whose ghost appeared to Macbeth? | In 'Hamlet', what was the name of Ophelia's father? | In 'The Winter's Tale', what made Leontes jealous? |
| In 'Macbeth', which wood came to Dunsinane Hill? | In 'Hamlet', who killed Polonius? | What spell was cast on Bottom? | Who killed Juliet's cousin Tybalt? | What was the name of the sprite who worked for Prospero? |

READ & RESPOND

Mr. William Shakespeare's Plays

# The Shakespeare Awards

● This is your chance to pick out some of the best bits of Shakespeare plays and give them special awards.

The award for nastiest villain goes to:

The award for funniest bit goes to:

The award for most bloodthirsty bit goes to:

The award for best ending goes to:

The award for funniest character goes to:

The award for funniest audience member goes to:

The award for saddest moment goes to:

The award for best play goes to:

Marcia Williams has written and illustrated a number of books that retell classic stories, ranging from the Greek myths to Don Quixote. In all her work, the use of illustration is dynamic: speech bubbles and illustrations interact with a narrative text. In *Mr. William Shakespeare's Plays*, Williams has provided a clear outline of seven Shakespeare plays. These incorporate dialogue from the original plays, and retain much of the plays' essential dramatic tension and humour.

## MANAGING THE READING OF *MR. WILLIAM SHAKESPEARE'S PLAYS*

The book is a retelling, and thus any study of it involves looking at the work of two authors: the creator of the plays, William Shakespeare; and the illustrator and author of the retelling, Marcia Williams.

The introductory activity and the three **Ways in** activities are designed to be carried out before the book is read. The first **Ways in** activity explores what the children already know about Shakespeare; the second opens up some of the possibilities presented by situations that will arise in the plays; and the third explores the presentation style of Marcia Williams' book.

The **Making sense** activities accompany the individual plays, with two photocopiables for each play. The plays and accompanying activities are:
• 'Romeo and Juliet' (pages 7 and 8 of this book)
• 'Hamlet' (pages 9 and 10)
• 'A Midsummer Night's Dream' (pages 11 and 12)
• 'Macbeth' (pages 13 and 14)
• 'The Winter's Tale' (pages 15 and 16)
• 'Julius Caesar' (pages 17 and 18)
• 'The Tempest' (pages 19 and 20).

The **Developing ideas** activities that follow look back over the plays. None of these activities focus solely on one play. They all involve elements of comparison, and require an overview of the whole book.

## CLASSROOM MANAGEMENT AND SUPPORT

*Mr. William Shakespeare's Plays* can be read by individuals, a group or the whole class. If the book is to be used in guided reading, it may be helpful for the teacher to give a brief outline of the main problems that the characters are facing in each story before leaving a group to read through to the conclusion.

The following activities will work better if done by pairs of children:
• **Making sense:** 'If only...' (page 7); 'Unhappy families' (page 10); 'Who loves who?' (page 11); 'Leontes' reactions' (page 16); 'Guess who?' (page 17); 'An argument' (page 18).
• **Developing ideas:** 'Character groups' (page 22); 'Common features' (page 23); 'A Shakespeare quiz' (page 25).

Some of the activities require children to reread a particular part of the book. These are marked with the icon 📖. It is advisable to invest in at least six copies of the book, so that groups and pairs can work independently. If a whole class is working on the book, plan the lesson so that some children are doing activities that require copies of the book while others are working on activities that can be done without direct access to the text.

Make sure you give the children ample opportunity to share and discuss their work, in groups or as a class.

## DIFFERENTIATION

Do not work slavishly through the activities in this book. Some of the **Making sense** activities might be better kept until the whole book has been completed and the children are ready to go back to a particular play and examine it in more depth.

All the activities are aimed at children in Years 5 and 6 (Primary 6 and 7 in Scotland). Their content relates to the learning objectives of the National Literacy Strategy. Many of the activities will also prove useful with Year 3 and Year 4 (Primary 4 and 5) classes. Teachers will need to plan to support children who may find some of the material difficult.

Each activity has a learning core which is stated as its 'Aim' in the **Teachers' notes** (pages 29–32). Children will achieve these aims to varying degrees. The more challenging activities include:
• **Making sense:** 'If only...' (page 7); 'Unhappy families' (page 10); 'Leontes' reactions' (page 16); 'Moment jigsaws' (page 20).

- **Developing ideas:** 'Lines and plays' (page 21); 'Common features' (page 23); 'A Shakespeare quiz' (page 25).

## TIMESCALE
The individual stories are best read one at a time, with gaps in between. Alongside the reading of each story there can be discussion of the events and characters, perhaps leading to a rereading of some sections.

## MATCHING THE BOOK TO YOUR CLASS
Marcia Williams' book works well with children at the top of Key Stage 2. However, the style in which the stories are presented makes them accessible to Years 3 and 4. In some cases, the teacher might choose a particular story for certain children. A story such as 'A Midsummer Night's Dream' is more accessible than one such as 'Julius Caesar'.

## TEACHING POTENTIAL OF *MR. WILLIAM SHAKESPEARE'S PLAYS*
The extension activities suggested in the **Teachers' notes** section (pages 29–32) indicate some of the potential that the text has for further work within the curriculum for English. There is much potential for cross-curricular links with history and geography – for example, project work on 'The Tudors' or 'The Romans'. There is also the potential for some interesting artwork in the style of Marcia Williams. For example, the children could draw their own stages for the telling of stories.

## GLOSSARY
During the activities, the following terms appear repeatedly. The children will need to be reminded of their meaning:
- **storyline:** the organization of events in a story
- **character:** a person who appears in a story
- **play:** a story presented in script form for acting
- **dialogue:** speech exchanged between characters.

## RECOMMENDED PREVIOUS TEACHING
Through prior teaching, the children should have encountered a range of characters and storylines. They should also be familiar with the way in which dialogue is organized in a play script.

## FURTHER READING
The following resources will be useful to support work with *Mr. William Shakespeare's Plays*:

**Background material**
*William Shakespeare* by Leon Ashworth (Cherrytree Books)
*The Terrible Tudors* by Terry Deary (Hippo)

**Other retellings of Shakespeare**
*Shakespeare Stories* and *Shakespeare Stories II* by Leon Garfield (Puffin)
*The Enchanted Island* by Ian Serraillier (Heinemann)

**...and the genuine article**
Throughout the reading of the book, it is worth having some copies of the original Shakespeare plays around. Children will sometimes want to have a look at certain speeches and scenes. The activity 'An argument' (page 18), where an edited version of a passage from 'Julius Caesar' is provided, could be applied to other plays.

**Other books by Marcia Williams**
*Greek Myths* (Walker)
*The Iliad and the Odyssey* (Walker)
*The Adventures of Robin Hood* (Walker)
*King Arthur and the Knights of the Round Table* (Walker)

**For teachers**
The ideas of story structure, plot and character are dealt with in *Reading and Responding to Fiction: Classroom Strategies for Developing Literacy* by Huw Thomas (Scholastic).

## INTRODUCTION
### MR. WILLIAM SHAKESPEARE'S PLAYS
*Aim:* to look at an author's comments on a book.
*Teaching points:* the comments from Marcia Williams can make interesting reading before the children start reading her versions of the plays. This activity, in conjunction with 'Mr William who?' (page 4), can lead the children to reflect on their prior knowledge of Shakepeare and the reactions that his name evokes.
*Extension:* As they read through the book, the children could draw up a list of further questions they would like to ask Marcia Williams.

## WAYS IN
### MR. WILLIAM WHO?
*Aim:* to begin to investigate the work of a famous author.
*Teaching points:* the prompt questions can be looked at by the children working in pairs or small groups. After reading these, the children can start to list what they know about an author with whom they may not be familiar. They may have heard his name, or know the name of one of his plays. You need to emphasize that any piece of relevant information is worth stating in this activity – even if it's just that Shakespeare was bald! It may be interesting to look at which responses are the most common. For example, certain well-known play titles or the fact that Shakespeare lived in Stratford may figure in more than one child's response.
*Extension:* the children could extend this to asking other people what they know about Shakespeare. They could ask other teachers or people at home.

### WHAT MIGHT HAPPEN?
*Aim:* to predict events in a narrative.
*Teaching points:* the seven scenarios outlined in this activity are quite open-ended. Without any knowledge of the plays, the children could come up with a range of possible outcomes. They should try to take account of the various parts of each scenario: for example, when they are asked to develop the idea 'a young girl falls in love with one of her father's enemies', they shouldn't just consider the love story. They need to include the father's views and deal with these within their development of the story.
*Extension:* the children can compare their outcomes as a group, looking at the variations for each scenario. The different versions can be recorded and referred to as each story is read, to see how the results of this exercise match up to the actual stories.

### MARCIA WILLIAMS' PAGES
*Aim:* to explore the style of an individual writer and illustrator.

*Teaching points:* Marcia Williams introduces her book with an outline of the way in which she has presented the plays. After reading this introduction, the children apply it to a particular play. This serves the dual purpose of preparing them for reading the text and helping them to identify the three aspects of the retelling. It also involves them in looking at the various layers of a particular text – a skill they will develop as they extend their reading experience.
*Extension:* the children could try producing their own pages in the style of Marcia Williams, presenting a scene from a novel they have read and incorporating the three aspects of the retelling.

## MAKING SENSE
### IF ONLY...
*Aim:* to experiment with alternative events in a storyline.
*Teaching points:* by looking at the various possibilities in the story of 'Romeo and Juliet', the children explore the overall way in which the story is structured. Narratives of this kind make their way through a network of possible outcomes, resulting in a tragic storyline. Encourage the children to list more than one simple result of each alternative. For example, if they think the parents would have been angry to hear of the two lovers' relationship, they can go on to consider what the outcome of this would have been. Would they have overcome their anger? Would the lovers have run away?
*Extension:* The children could script a scene based on one of the alternative storylines they have devised.

### VERONA TIMES
*Aim:* to investigate the presentation of characters.
*Teaching points:* adopting the viewpoints of three characters, the children can respond to the questions and, in doing so, flesh out the thoughts and feelings of these characters. The activity could lead to follow-up questions from other children in the group. The children may also want to discuss whether the response a particular child gives (in role) is the one that the character would actually have given.
*Extension:* having collated information from the interview, the children could write a news report and decide which 'soundbites' they would use if they were presenting a *Verona News* television report.

### TROUBLE AT ELSINORE
*Aim:* to look at an aspect of a story from the viewpoints of different characters.
*Teaching points:* Hamlet appears as a complex character to anyone reading the whole story (let

alone the play). In this activity, the children have to take a step further into the story and consider how the other characters would feel about Hamlet. Stress to the children that they do not need to stick to the words in the book: they can express the responses of different characters in their own words.
*Extension:* this activity could lead to an exploration of the feelings between any two of these characters. What, for example, might Gertrude think of Ophelia?

## UNHAPPY FAMILIES
*Aim:* to explore a complex narrative.
*Teaching points:* part of the complexity of a play such as 'Hamlet' lies in the different relationships between the characters. In this activity, the children have to unpick complex family and other relationships in order to judge the accuracy of the statements provided. This requires them to look closely through the events of the story. It also brings home the variety of loyalties and betrayals in the story, as brothers defend sisters and sons argue with mothers. As they read through the statements, the children should be encouraged to make a note of which characters are being referred to above each statement.
*Extension:* the children could try drawing a 'family tree' type of diagram, showing the various characters and their relationships.

## WHO LOVES WHO?
*Aim:* to examine relationships between characters.
*Teaching points:* as a way of understanding how the 'love' relationships develop in 'A Midsummer Night's Dream', the children use the question board to construct various questions such as the one shown in the example. They then need to look through the whole story to find out whether there is a point at which they can answer 'yes'. In looking at the questions in this way, the children will have to review the ways in which different relationships between characters form and change throughout the story.
*Extension:* the children could make a list of who was in love with whom in the story. They could then try to distinguish romantic attachments that happened as a result of the magic flower and ones that happened for other reasons.

## MAGIC FLOWER
*Aim:* to explore a theme in a particular story.
*Teaching points:* The theme of magic underpins the story of 'A Midsummer Night's Dream'. As

they read through the story, the children can look at the various uses to which magic is put. There are four uses: three to create new loves and one to restore an old love. Once they have found each of the uses of magic, the children could also put a number on each flower petal to show the order in which these events occurred.
*Extension:* at the end of the story, one of the uses of magic has not been undone. Can the children say which one?

## BAD TO WORSE
*Aim:* to explore the plot structure of a story.
*Teaching points:* as well as being a sequencing activity, the ordering of these events presents the children with a stark overview of the tragic way in which Macbeth's life is going well at first, but then goes steadily from bad to worse. They will also be drawn to find connections between some of these events. For example, the order in which the two events that involve Macduff are placed has a certain logic.
*Extension:* the children could try looking for other significant events that can be added to the sequence.

## AUDIENCE COMMENTS
*Aim:* to explore potential responses that a story could evoke in readers.
*Teaching points:* part of this activity is a search for the responses shown in the speech bubbles, but the most important aspect of it is the linking of each response to the story being acted out. The children need to look at how the events of the play lead to the responses shown. Obviously, these are fictitious responses to the play; but the children can evaluate them nonetheless. They could look at whether the audience member is enjoying the play or has understood the story. What does the response tell us about the person who is making it?
*Extension:* the children could follow this up by looking at illustrations from stories they know and writing a set of 'audience reactions' in speech bubbles around the page.

## A CAST LIST
*Aim:* to investigate the representation of particular characters.
*Teaching points:* this activity must follow an initial reading of the story. Using the activity page, the children review the actions or traits of the various characters. Point out that some characters will reappear at different points throughout the story, so they will need to consider carefully where they

select their character comment from. Different comments may be true of the same character at different times; the children can choose what points they feel are most significant.

*Extension:* the children's responses could be collected into a folder. The children could then work in eight small groups, each group looking at all the comments on a particular character. From this survey, they could present an overview to the class of the opinions formed about that character.

### LEONTES' REACTIONS

*Aim:* to investigate the actions of a particular character.

*Teaching points:* by focusing on one aspect of Leontes' behaviour (his reactions to events and pieces of news), the children can build up a picture of his personality. Point out the way in which he reacts negatively to all the things that readers might expect him to be pleased by, such as the news of Perdita's birth and the Oracle's verdict. Why do they think he behaves like this?

*Extension:* having formed their own impression of Leontes, the children could review the ways in which audience members react to him in Marcia Williams' version.

### GUESS WHO?

*Aims:* To find answers to questions by reading a story. To examine character roles.

*Teaching points:* as the children read the story of 'Julius Caesar', they will encounter a large number of characters. It can be difficult to follow who is who in a story of this kind. One way in which the children can work out who did each of the listed actions is by a process of elimination. If, for example, the question asks 'Who quarrelled with Brutus?', they will see that 'Brutus' is an unlikely answer. They may also recall that Caesar and Brutus did not quarrel, and dismiss Portia as a possibility. As they eliminate names in this way, they draw closer to the actual answer.

*Extension:* the children could use these questions for a quiz. One child could act as question master, putting the 'Guess who?' questions to two teams who take turns to answer.

### AN ARGUMENT

*Aim:* to explore different versions of the same story.

*Teaching points:* the passage of dialogue provided is an abridged version of Shakespeare's text. Looking through this script, the children should be able to recognize the scene from the Marcia Williams version of the play and pick out the lines she has used in her illustration. They should also be able to see this episode in the context of the whole story – for example, understanding the references to Antony and Octavius. You can

suggest other aspects of the argument they could look out for in this script, such as the sarcastic remark about flattery. Unfamiliar words can be listed, and the children can try guessing their meanings from the context.

*Extension:* the children could try learning and acting out part of the argument, with tempers rising and feelings being expressed!

### POINTS OF VIEW

*Aim:* to examine character viewpoints and relationships.

*Teaching points:* throughout 'The Tempest', the relationships between the characters are evolving. In this activity, the children investigate the relationships that exist between various characters. An initial discussion may help to draw the children into the activity. They should be left to decide which part of the play they will draw on as material for their evaluation. For example, Alonso's view of Prospero will depend on whether the children focus on the early part or the ending of the play.

*Extension:* as a short drama activity, pairs of children could take up the pairings suggested and act out 'head to head' conversations between these characters, using dialogue from the play and imagining more things the characters would say to each other.

### MOMENT JIGSAWS

*Aim:* to identify the key features of a narrative text.

*Teaching points:* in this activity, each of several key events in 'The Tempest' is shown as two separate 'jigsaw pieces' of information: cause and effect. As they reunite the halves, the children will be making links that form much of the plot. The idea of one thing leading to another is crucial in the plotting of stories. In some of the halves, the children will have to identify characters who are represented only by pronouns. For example, when a jigsaw piece says 'Stefano fell over them', the children have to identify the 'them' of this clause by matching to the first half of the sentence.

*Extension:* the children could make four-piece jigsaws that join together longer sequences of linked events in 'The Tempest'; then they could try representing other plays in this way.

### DEVELOPING IDEAS
### LINES AND PLAYS

*Aim:* to explore the use of language in older literature.

*Teaching points:* this activity involves a search through the plays to find particular lines. Within the lines given, there are clues as to which story they come from: character names or references to particular events. To understand the meanings of these quotes, the children will have to look at the overall plot of the story and work out how each piece of dialogue fits in. This involves thinking about Shakespeare's use of language: the ways in which particular lines express ideas and feelings.

*Extension:* the children could devise their own 'line search', using other lines from the plays. They could test each other – or you.

### CHARACTER GROUPS

*Aim:* to identify characters as belonging to different stories.

*Teaching points:* the list of character names provided includes three characters from each Shakespeare play in the book. The children should initially try to sort them without looking at the book. They can then go through the plays to check the accuracy of their sorting work.

*Extension:* the children could go on to sort the same characters according to their own criteria. For example, they might sort characters with magic powers from ones without.

### COMMON FEATURES

*Aim:* to compare different stories and identify recurring features.

*Teaching points:* in this activity, the children look for recurring elements in the plays. As they do this, they will begin to see how common themes, such as magic and parental conflicts, permeate these stories. They could also be encouraged to look at features in the plays that are **similar** to the ones listed in this exercise. For example: although he is not a king, Caesar is a murdered ruler; and although he is not murdered, Prospero is a ruler who is forced out of power.

*Extension:* the children could check through all the plays and decide how many of the common features listed appear in each play. As above, they could look out for features similar to those listed.

### STAGES AND BALCONIES

*Aim:* to adapt the ideas of another author in writing.

*Teaching points:* adapting the style of Marcia Williams, the children can use these spaces to create their own scenes from Shakespeare plays. They can choose how much to copy from the book and how much to invent. The balcony spaces should be filled in after the children have looked through the book to see the kind of comments made by the audience members. These may be sympathetic or unsympathetic to characters in the play; express something about the audience

member's own background; or refer to similarities between the play in progress and other narratives.

*Extensions:* using another copy of this page, the children could create scenes from other stories as if acted out on a stage, with new audience comments. The stories could be adapted from Greek myths, Biblical parables or modern children's literature.

The children could discuss what the book would be like without the audience. They are not essential to a grasp of the plays, so what do they add to the book? Could the children think of ways to include the voices of readers in some of their own story writing?

As a fun activity, the children could play 'Where's Willy?' – a game modelled on the popular 'Where's Wally?' pictures. In each of the plays, Shakespeare appears in the audience, holding a quill pen. Working in pairs, the children could try to find him in each play and note the scene to which he is closest.

### A SHAKESPEARE QUIZ

*Aim:* to recall and research information from stories.

*Teaching points:* the quiz is designed to provide a mix of questions referring to each of the plays. In some cases, it is clear from the question which play is referred to. In others, the children need to relate a character name to a play in order to think of the answer. The quiz game is best played on more than one occasion, with children attempting it after they have researched those questions that they struggled with the first time. As their scores rise, some teams may become more and more motivated to be the ones who can answer every question!

*Extension:* the children could add to the set of question cards, devising their own questions about what happens in the Shakespeare plays.

### EVALUATION
### THE SHAKESPEARE AWARDS

*Aim:* to express preferences in response to literature.

*Teaching points:* the certificates in this activity invite the children to make value judgements about characters and events in the stories. They should be encouraged to record notes on why they chose a particular winner for each category. What was it, for example, that led them to decide a particular villain was the nastiest?

*Extension:* these certificates could form the basis of a class poll among the children to find the overall winner in each category.